Saint Catherine Labouré

And Our Lady of the Miraculous Medal

Written by Marianne Lorraine Trouvé, FSP

Illustrated by Cathy Morrison

D1607968

Pauline

BOOKS & MEDIA

Boston

Library of Congress Cataloging-in-Publication Data

Trouvé, Marianne Lorraine.

 Saint Catherine Labouré : And Our Lady of the Miraculous Medal / Written by Marianne Lorraine Trouvé, FSP ; Illustrated by Cathy Morrison.

     pages cm -- (Encounter the Saints)
  ISBN-13: 978-0-8198-7224-1
  ISBN-10: 0-8198-7224-5
  1. Labouré, Catherine, Saint, 1806-1876--Juvenile literature. 2. Christian saints--France--Biography--Juvenile literature. 3. Christian women saints--France--Biography--Juvenile literature. 4. Miraculous Medal--Juvenile literature. I. Morrison, Cathy, illustrator. II. Title.
  BX4700.L2T76 2012
  282.092--dc23
  [B]

                    2011052916

Book design by Mary Joseph Peterson, FSP

Cover art and illustrations by Cathy Morrison

"P" and PAULINE are registered trademarks of the Daughters of St. Paul.

Published by Pauline Books & Media, 50 Saint Pauls Avenue, Boston, MA 02130-3491

Printed in the U.S.A.

SCL VSAUSAPEOILL1-3J12-01088 7224-5

www.pauline.org

Pauline Books & Media is the publishing house of the Daughters of St. Paul, an international congregation of women religious serving the Church with the communications media.

1 2 3 4 5 6 7 8 9   16 15 14 13 12

Encounter the Saints Series

Blesseds Jacinta and Francisco Marto
Shepherds of Fatima

Blessed John Paul II
The People's Pope

Blessed Pier Giorgio Frassati
Journey to the Summit

Blessed Teresa of Calcutta
Missionary of Charity

Journeys with Mary
Apparitions of Our Lady

Saint Anthony of Padua
Fire and Light

Saint Bakhita of Sudan
Forever Free

Saint Bernadette Soubirous
And Our Lady of Lourdes

Saint Catherine Labouré
And Our Lady of the Miraculous Medal

Saint Clare of Assisi
A Light for the World

Saint Damien of Molokai
Hero of Hawaii

Saint Edith Stein
Blessed by the Cross

Saint Elizabeth Ann Seton
Daughter of America

Saint Faustina Kowalska
Messenger of Mercy

Saint Frances Xavier Cabrini
Cecchina's Dream

Saint Francis of Assisi
Gentle Revolutionary

Saint Gianna Beretta Molla
The Gift of Life

Saint Ignatius of Loyola
For the Greater Glory of God

Saint Isaac Jogues
With Burning Heart

Saint Joan of Arc
God's Soldier

Saint John Vianney
A Priest for All People

Saint Juan Diego
And Our Lady of Guadalupe

Saint Katharine Drexel
The Total Gift

Saint Martin de Porres
Humble Healer

Saint Maximilian Kolbe
Mary's Knight

Saint Paul
The Thirteenth Apostle

Saint Pio of Pietrelcina
Rich in Love

Saint Teresa of Avila
Joyful in the Lord

Saint Thérèse of Lisieux
The Way of Love

For other children's titles on the saints, visit our Web site:
www.pauline.org.

CONTENTS

Prologue 1

1. Life on the Farm 3

2. A New Role 9

3. A Growing Desire 15

4. Following a Dream 19

5. Rue du Bac 25

6. The Lady 31

7. A Special Mission 37

8. Back to the Farm 43

9. The Medal 49

10. Miracles 55

11. Catherine's Secret 61

12. Ordinary Life 65

13. Fire! 69

14. Another Mission for Father Aladel 75

15. The War 83

16. More Trouble 87

17. Into Flight 93

18. Back to Normal 97

19. Some Changes 101

20. The Final Road 107

Prayer 113

Glossary 115

PROLOGUE

After a full day of work on the family farm, Catherine tumbled into bed and fell fast asleep. She started dreaming. The vivid images of her dream showed Catherine the parish church in her hometown of Fain les Moutiers (pronounced *fahn lay MOO-tee-ay*). She was praying in the Lady chapel (the chapel dedicated to the Blessed Mother). It was also called the Labouré chapel, named for her family because they had paid for repair work that it had needed.

As she was praying, she saw an old priest come into the chapel and go to the altar. He had a short beard and a kind-hearted face. He was wearing white vestments. Facing the altar, he started to celebrate the Mass. (At Catherine's time, priests didn't face the people but the altar during Mass. They also used Latin for the prayers of the Mass.) Before the opening prayer, he turned around and said, *"Dominus vobiscum!"* which means "The Lord be with you." As the old priest said this, he looked straight at

Catherine. She felt that he could see straight into her heart.

The Mass continued. At the end of Mass, the old priest turned around and looked at Catherine. He beckoned to her, as if he wanted to tell her something, but she drew back, unsure, and left the church.

As the dream unfolded, Catherine found herself at the bedside of a sick woman, helping to take care of her. Suddenly, the mysterious priest was there again! He was wearing a black cap on his head. Catherine was confused. What was going on? Then the elderly priest smiled at her and said, "My daughter, it's good to care for the sick. God has plans for you. Don't forget it!" Then he vanished, and Catherine walked home.

Catherine woke up abruptly. She remembered every detail of the dream, but most of all, the old priest's words: "God has plans for you." She still didn't know what this meant, but she felt happy. She thought about her life and pondered those words, "God has plans for you." What could it mean?

1

Life on the Farm

"Come on, Zoe, let's feed the pigeons!" Tonine (pronounced *TWA-neen*) Labouré tugged at her sister's sleeve. Two years older than Tonine, nine-year-old Catherine was often called Zoe, after the saint on whose feast day she had been born. Catherine had entered the world on May 2, 1806.

"All right, Tonine, let's get some grain." The girls lived on a big farm with their parents and eight brothers and sisters. Their farm was located in the small town of Fain les Moutiers, in a part of France called Burgundy. Catherine loved to feed the animals and run through the fields on the farm, but her favorite place was the large building for the pigeons. The Labouré family had more than 600 pigeons, which they used for food and sold at the market.

The girls filled their aprons with grain and went to feed the birds. "Watch out, Tonine, here they come!" The girls threw the grain up into the air and laughed with delight as the birds swooped down to get something to eat. They flapped their wings and cooed as they competed for the grain. But Catherine spread it out generously, making sure they all had enough.

She was always that way, generous with others. She kept special watch over her little brother Auguste. A few years earlier, he had fallen out of a cart and hurt his legs. From then on he was crippled. Catherine always took good care of him and made sure he was included in everything.

Early on the morning of October 9, 1815, sadness came over the Labouré household. Catherine's mother, Madeleine, was dying. Pierre Labouré, Catherine's father, kept watch by his wife's side. One by one, the ten children of the Labouré family came into the room and gathered around her bed.

Catherine started to cry. As the tears rolled down her cheeks, the family recited prayers for the dying. Quietly her mother slipped away from earth.

"Mama, Mama!" Catherine cried out. Then she ran out of the room, sobbing. The other children were all crying too.

Later, Catherine came back to her mother's room. She saw a statue of our Blessed Mother Mary on top of a piece of furniture. Catherine couldn't reach it, so she got a chair and stood on it. Reaching up, she hugged the statue and prayed to Mary, "Now you will be my mother!" In her heart Catherine felt a sense of warmth and protection, and she knew that Mary would always look after her.

What would happen now? Her father couldn't take care of the farm and of all the children by himself. Some of the older boys had already left the farm, seeking their own way in the world. Even so, Pierre needed help. So he called Catherine and said, "Catherine, I want to send you and your sister Tonine to your Aunt Marguerite. She lives in Saint Rémy (pronounced *sahn RAY-mee*), only five miles away. She will take care of you and be like a mother to you."

Catherine's face fell. "But Father, I don't want to be away from you. I'd rather stay here with you."

Pierre's eyes filled with tears. "I know, my little one. I would much rather have you stay with me. But I just can't handle everything right now. You need a mother."

Sadly, Catherine agreed. She couldn't do much else. So she and Tonine went to their aunt's house. Her aunt had six children of her own, so Catherine and Tonine were mostly left to themselves. The maid took care of them, but it wasn't like having a mother. It was hard.

Finally, after two years, Catherine's father sent word for them to come back home. Catherine was overjoyed. She and Tonine went back to the farm.

Good news awaited Catherine upon her return home.

"Catherine, it's time for you to make your first Communion," her father told her. "You are old enough now."

Catherine's eyes lit up. "When will that be, Father?"

"In a few months," Pierre replied.

To prepare for this special day, Catherine received some lessons. She didn't know how to read or write. Her mother had wanted to teach her, but with all the farm work to take care of, she hadn't been able to.

So Catherine memorized her lessons. She understood that when she received Communion, she would receive the Body and Blood of Jesus Christ.

The great day arrived—January 25, 1818. Catherine went to church, dressed in her finest clothes. During the Mass, she told Jesus, "I want to receive you so much, Lord. Thank you for coming to me!" After she received our Lord, she prayed with all her heart and told Jesus how much she loved him. Something special stirred in her heart that day. It was the beginning of a desire to give herself completely to Jesus.

But for now, the farm awaited her.

2

A NEW ROLE

While she was away, Catherine's oldest sister, Marie Louise, had helped to take care of all the farm work. But she had a dream for her life and was about to fulfill it. One day while the family was together, Marie Louise brought up the subject.

"Father," she began, "I have to tell you something that I want very much."

"What is it?" he asked.

"For a long time now I have been thinking about becoming a Daughter of Charity. I want to help the poor and give my life to God."

"But what about the farm?" he asked. "I still need your help to run it and get all the work done."

Marie Louise looked at Catherine. "Well, Father, I was thinking that Catherine is back home now . . ." she began.

"Catherine? But she is only twelve years old!" Pierre protested.

Catherine sat up attentively. She listened and then thought things over. After a little while, she spoke up.

"I can help take care of the farm!" she announced.

A surprised look spread over her father's face. "What! Do you really think you can?" he asked her.

"Yes!" she replied. "Tonine and I will be able to manage!"

Her father thought for a while. Then he said, "Well, if you are willing, I will let you. Then Marie Louise can go to the Daughters of Charity."

So it all worked out. Catherine took over running the farm. Her father was still in charge, but he couldn't manage it by himself. He gave Catherine the freedom to run things. They had workers who helped in the fields, and Catherine was in charge of them all!

Catherine arose at four every morning. "Thank you for this day, Lord!" she whispered as she climbed out of bed.

She washed, dressed, and headed out to milk the cows. She brought the fresh milk inside and prepared breakfast for everyone.

"I can help take care of the farm!" she announced.

"Tonine, will you help me feed the animals?" Catherine asked after breakfast.

The two girls washed the breakfast dishes and skipped outside. After feeding the animals, Catherine collected the eggs that the hens had laid and brought water from the well. Soon it was time to cook lunch.

"Here comes Catherine!" one of the workers called. All the field hands stopped working and gathered around Catherine. Each day, she brought lunch to the field for the workers.

"What a good cook she is!" one of them said as he ate. "And she is so kind!"

After lunch, Catherine continued to work: gathering firewood, helping in the garden, doing laundry, and baking bread. After supper, she joined the family for night prayers; then she pulled out her sewing.

"Will you go to the market tomorrow, Catherine?" her father asked her.

"Yes, tomorrow is Thursday, market day," Catherine replied. "We have lots of vegetables to sell. And I'm sure to meet other farmers and get new ideas from them."

Even with all the work she was doing, Catherine managed to find time for more prayer. Whenever she could, she would go to the village church to pray. She loved these special times of silence, when she would quietly tell Jesus everything in her heart.

On Sundays, Catherine and Tonine walked to Mass together. No priest lived in their own town, so they walked about three miles to the next town of Moutiers-Saint-Jean (pronounced *MOO-tee-ay sahn JHAH*). They talked and laughed as they traveled along the beautiful country road.

Sometimes Catherine went to Mass during the week, too. She would walk to Moutiers-Saint-Jean and go to the chapel of the Daughters of Charity. After Mass one day she stopped to talk to one of the sisters.

"What do you do all day, Sister Soucial (pronounced *SOO-see-al*)?" Catherine asked with curiosity.

"We take care of the needs of poor people. We feed them, clothe them, and go visit the sick. Saint Vincent de Paul often said, 'The poor have much to teach you. You have much to learn from them.'"

"That sounds like a beautiful way to live. My older sister Marie Louise left home to join your community. Sometimes she writes, but I don't hear from her much. I just wanted to find out more about your life."

Sister Soucial smiled. Then she added, "We also pray for everyone. Prayer is so important. God knows how to help those whom we can't help."

"I must get back home now," Catherine said. "There's a lot of work waiting for me!"

As she walked back home, she thought about what the sister had said. Something was stirring in Catherine's heart.

3

A GROWING DESIRE

Life continued as usual, but Catherine
was different now. She was growing up. She
excelled at managing the farm, but she
desired more. She never forgot her vivid
dream with the old priest who had spoken
to her. What did those strange words mean,
"God has plans for you?"

On the weekdays when she went to Mass
at the sisters' chapel, she spent more and
more time speaking to the sisters afterward,
and she learned about their way of life.
Little by little, she found herself feeling
drawn to them. She was seriously thinking
about becoming a Daughter of Charity. But
there was a problem. Catherine had never
gone to school, so she still didn't know how
to read and write even though she was eighteen.

How was Catherine going to learn to
read and write? God made a way for her.
She had a cousin on her mother's side of the
family, Antoinette Gontard (pronounced
AHN-twa-net GŌN-tar), who ran a boarding

school in the city of Châtillon (pronounced *SHA-tee-own*). Antoinette agreed to take Catherine on as a student. Catherine was excited about this opportunity and obtained her father's permission to attend school.

While she was there, Catherine was often able to go to Mass at a nearby church. This made her very happy. The priest there was named Abbé Gailhac (pronounced *ah-BAY GUY-ac*). He was in his eighties. One day Catherine decided to confide in him, telling him about her dream. She still wondered what it might mean. After she had told him about the old priest in her dream and what he had said, the Abbé told her, "My child, I think that this priest must have been Saint Vincent de Paul!"

Catherine replied, "Saint Vincent? The priest who founded the Daughters of Charity?"

"Yes," the Abbé told her. "None other than he."

Shortly after this, Antoinette took Catherine to visit the Daughters of Charity nearby. As they were waiting in the reception room, Catherine noticed a portrait of an old priest. He looked just like the one she had seen in her dream!

When some of the sisters came to greet them, Catherine asked, "Who is that priest in the portrait?"

The sisters told her, "That is our father, Saint Vincent de Paul!"

The Abbé had been right! The priest that Catherine had seen in her dream was Saint Vincent! Was God using Saint Vincent to confirm Catherine's desire to become a Daughter of Charity?

4

FOLLOWING A DREAM

In the school at Châtillon, Catherine was learning how to read and write, but she did not feel comfortable there. She was eighteen, much older than the other students, who were still little girls. She felt awkward and out of place.

After two years she decided to go back home, to the farm in Fain les Moutiers. She had always loved taking care of the farm, the animals, and the garden, but now she kept thinking about her dream of Saint Vincent. More and more, the desire to become a Daughter of Charity grew in her heart, but she faced one obstacle. She knew that her father would oppose her desire. He still needed her to run the farm. So Catherine decided to wait until she was twenty-one, when she would legally be an adult.

On her twenty-first birthday, Catherine approached her father. He was sitting in his favorite chair in the kitchen. "Father," Catherine began, "I have something important to speak to you about."

"What is it?" he replied.

"For some time now I have been thinking about what to do with my life," she said.

"Ah, yes," Pierre said, "you are now at an age when you should marry."

Catherine sighed. This was going to be difficult. "Father, I'm not thinking about getting married." She could see the frown on his face.

"Then what are you thinking about?" he asked.

Catherine knew she might as well come right to the point. "I want to become a Daughter of Charity."

"A Daughter of Charity? But I've already given one of my daughters to God. Marie Louise has been a sister for many years now."

"Yes, but God is calling me too. I want to help the poor, the sick, and those who can't take care of themselves," Catherine told him.

Pierre Labouré grew very quiet. Finally he said, "Catherine, several young men are interested in marrying you. You would be able to find a good husband and have a good life as a wife and mother. I think that's what you should do."

But Catherine was as determined as her father. She told him, "For now I will wait, but I know that God is calling me to be a Daughter of Charity. I don't want to turn God down!"

So Catherine continued her life on the farm. About a year later the family got some sad news. Catherine's brother Charles had gone to Paris, gotten married, and started a restaurant business. But then his young wife died. They had only been married for two years. Charles asked if Catherine could come to Paris to help him run the restaurant. Although this work was not to her liking, she agreed and went to help him. Just as she had done on the farm, she worked hard at the restaurant. Some of the young men who came in noticed Catherine and wanted to get to know her more, but her heart was set on becoming a Daughter of Charity.

On February 3, 1829, Charles remarried. Now that he had a wife, Catherine felt she could leave. She wrote to her oldest sister, Marie Louise, who was a Daughter of Charity. Catherine told her she wanted to become a sister. Marie Louise was very happy to hear this, but she told Catherine that she still needed more education. So Catherine asked her cousin Antoinette if she could go back to the boarding school. Antoinette agreed. Catherine was once again a student in Châtillon.

She studied hard, eager to learn as much as she could. Catherine often went to visit the nearby house of the Daughters of Charity. She got to know a young sister there, Sister Victoire Séjoule (pronounced *VICK-twa SAY-jool*). Sister Victoire was just a few years older than Catherine, and they became friends. They had many things in common. Catherine told Sister Victoire that she wanted to become a Daughter of Charity. Sister Victoire went to talk to Sister Cany (pronounced *KA-nee*), who was the superior.

"Catherine wants to become a Daughter of Charity," she began.

"Does she love the poor?" Sister Cany asked.

"Yes," Sister Victoire replied, "very much so. And she loves the Blessed Mother too. She comes from a farm and knows how to work hard."

Sister Cany said, "I have seen her and I like her. She has what it takes to be a good Daughter of Charity. But I am concerned about her lack of education."

"It is true that she is not well educated," Sister Victoire replied, "but she doesn't feel at home at the boarding school. The others are so much younger than she is, and they come from the city. Catherine is a country girl. If she enters now, I will teach her everything she needs to know!"

When Sister Victoire saw Catherine, she told her, "Sister Cany is sending a letter to the motherhouse in Paris to ask permission for you to enter!"

Catherine was thrilled. "But will they say yes?" she asked.

Sister Victoire replied, "Let's hope and pray they will!"

5

Rue du Bac

For the next few weeks, Catherine found it hard to concentrate on her studies. She kept wondering, "Will they say yes?" Finally one day when she went to visit the sisters, Sister Victoire met Catherine.

"I have some good news for you!" she said. Then, with a big smile, she added, "The answer is yes! You have received permission to join us!"

Catherine beamed with excitement. "Thank you! I also thank our Lord and our Blessed Mother Mary! I know that she offered my prayers to Jesus!"

After that, things happened in a whirlwind. Catherine prepared the things that she would need. She entered the Daughters of Charity toward the end of January 1830, in their house in Châtillon. Catherine was a postulant—someone who is trying to find out if God is calling her to the religious life.

Sister Victoire taught Catherine more about prayer. She also taught her about the different ways the Daughters of Charity served the poor. Twice a week they prepared a large amount of soup to feed the poor. People came with containers to take it away and give it to others.

"Catherine," Sister Victoire said after a few months, "it is time for you to go to our motherhouse in Paris."

"Paris?" asked Catherine.

"Yes," Sister Victoire replied. "You will begin your novitiate there."

Novitiate was the time when Catherine would learn more about prayer and service to the poor. It was a time to get to know Jesus more deeply through prayer and meditation. She also had a lot to learn about the religious life and life as a Daughter of Charity. So in April 1830 she went to Paris, about 200 miles away. The sisters' house was located on a street called Rue du Bac (pronounced *ROO doo BAHK*). Catherine didn't know it yet, but she would make that street famous!

In the novitiate, Catherine followed a strict schedule. She and the other sisters got up at four o'clock in the morning, but she was already used to that from the farm. Their day was filled with work, study, and prayer. First thing in the morning, Catherine went to the chapel with the other sisters for prayers and Mass.

After breakfast—usually bread and a soup made from milk—the novices had some classes to help them learn the faith better. Then they had time for various chores: peeling vegetables, cooking, sewing, and laundry.

One day one of the sisters told Catherine, "Something special will be happening soon! The relics of Saint Vincent de Paul have been kept in the bishop's house for a while. But now he wants to return them to the Vincentian priests."

Relics are objects kept as a remembrance of a saint. They are either from the body itself, or from things the saint owned during life. In this case, the body of Saint Vincent was kept as a remembrance of him. It was enclosed in a special container called a reliquary.

"When will the relics be moved?" Catherine asked.

"Next Sunday, April 25. A procession will take place, and all of the novices will be able to join!"

So that Sunday, Catherine joined the huge crowd of sisters and other people. The procession behind Saint Vincent's relics wound slowly through the streets of Paris. It ended at the church of Saint Lazare. This church was run by the Vincentian priests, and was very close to the sisters' motherhouse on Rue du Bac.

The celebrations didn't end there. They continued for a whole week. Every day, Catherine went to pray before the relics of Saint Vincent. Many years later, she would say that she had asked the saint to obtain many graces for her, for the sisters and priests in the family of Saint Vincent, and for all the people of France.

During that week, something amazing happened. In their chapel on Rue du Bac, the sisters had a small shrine in honor of Saint Vincent. Here they also had some of the saint's relics. One day as Catherine was praying there, she had a vision of Saint Vincent's heart. The vision happened three times—each time after she came back from praying before the relics of Saint Vincent at the church of Saint Lazare. The first time, his heart appeared white. The second time, it was a vivid red. The third time, his heart appeared much darker, in a sort of red-black color.

Later, Catherine understood that the white heart was a sign of peace and calmness. The bright red heart signified fervor, zeal, and charity. The darker, red-black heart made Catherine sad. She understood it to be a sign of troubles that would later come to France.

At the time, however, Catherine didn't know what to make of all this. She was troubled by it. So she decided to tell it to Father Aladel (pronounced *AH-la-del*), the Vincentian priest who heard the confessions of the sisters. He said, "Don't pay any attention to these things. Just forget about them. A Daughter of Charity is not supposed to dream but to serve the poor."

Catherine took to heart what he said and tried to forget about it, but she couldn't, because something else happened.

At Mass, after the consecration, when the bread becomes the Body of Christ, Catherine was startled to actually see Jesus in the host. He was dressed like a king, with the cross on his chest. This happened several times. Again, Catherine went to Father Aladel, but he told her the same thing, "Forget about these visions! It's just your imagination running wild!"

Catherine tried to follow his advice. It wasn't like her to dream up things. All of her work on the farm had made her very practical. She was a down-to-earth sort of person. So what could it all mean?

6

THE LADY

It was July 18, 1830. The next day would be the feast day of Saint Vincent. Catherine fell fast asleep, tired out from studying, praying, cleaning, and cooking.

At about eleven thirty at night, she suddenly heard someone calling her. "Sister Catherine! Sister Catherine! Get up!"

She started to sit up. She was surprised to see a small child, dressed all in white. The child said, "Get up right away and come to the chapel. The Blessed Virgin is waiting for you!"

Catherine thought, *Someone will hear me.*

But the child told her, "Don't be afraid. It's late and everyone is sound asleep. Come, I will wait for you."

Catherine quickly got dressed and followed the child. He led her to the chapel. On the way there, Catherine was surprised to see all the lights on. It was strange for them to be on so late. When they got to the chapel, the child merely put his fingertip on the heavy door and it swung open.

All the lights were on in the chapel too. The candles were burning. It looked like it was ready for a solemn Mass, like midnight Mass on Christmas. Mystified, Catherine followed the child who led her to the big chair where the priest sat for Mass. It was in the sanctuary, the part of the chapel near the altar. Catherine knelt down, and the little child stood near her. It seemed like a long time before anything happened.

Suddenly, the child cried out, "Here is the Blessed Virgin! Here she is!"

Catherine heard some noise. It sounded like the rustling of a silk dress. A beautiful lady appeared! Catherine was awestruck. The lady sat down on a chair nearby. But Catherine didn't believe it was the Blessed Mother.

As if to chide her for her doubt, the child said, "There is the Blessed Virgin!"

Catherine still didn't move.

The child cried a third time, "Here is the Blessed Virgin!"

Then Catherine rushed to be close to Mary. Catherine knelt right next to her, and she rested her hands on Mary's lap!

Our Lady smiled at Catherine and began to speak to her. Catherine later said it was the most beautiful moment she had ever experienced. Mary spent a long time speaking to her, telling Catherine how to be a good sister and how to become holy. Then Mary said to her, "My child, the good God wants to give you a mission! You will have many things to suffer. But you will rise above them because what you do is for God's glory. You will see some special things. They will trouble you until you tell your spiritual director. You will be contradicted. But do not be afraid! You will have grace."

Catherine began to wonder what this all meant. Her spiritual director, Father Aladel, heard her confessions and gave her advice on how to grow closer to God. Catherine knew it would be important to tell him about the vision later. Father Aladel was a wise and holy priest. He would be able to help Catherine figure out how to handle this. The vision continued. Catherine was so happy to see Mary. It was like talking to her best friend.

But then Mary's face grew sad. She had some bad news to tell Catherine. "Bad times will come. France will suffer hard times. The throne will be cast down. The whole world will be turned upside down by misfortunes of every kind."

*"My child, the good God wants
to give you a mission!"*

Catherine understood that Mary was speaking about Charles X, the king of France at that time. He was forced to step down from the throne just a few weeks later, on August 2, 1830. Political unrest swept through France.

As she said these things, Mary's face grew even sadder. She looked so full of sorrow!

Then Mary turned a little and pointed to the altar with her left hand. She said, "Come to the foot of this altar. There, graces will be poured out on everyone who asks for them with confidence and fervor."

Catherine took it all in. Later she would write down what Mary had told her.

Then our Lady talked to Catherine about her religious community. She made some recommendations as to what they could do better. Then she told Catherine, "Another community will ask to be joined to your community. I love this community and God will bless all of you. You will have great peace."

What Mary said here came true in 1850. Saint Elizabeth Ann Seton started her own community of sisters in the United States. She asked to join the family of Saint Vincent de Paul and unite her community with

Catherine's. And it happened, just as Mary said!

Mary continued to speak to Catherine about some other sad things that would happen in France later on. She told Catherine, "I myself will be with you. I have always watched over you. I will give you many graces. At the time when it seems all will be lost, I will be with you. Have great trust! Your community will have the protection of God and of Saint Vincent. Have confidence!"

Finally, the Blessed Virgin Mary finished speaking. Catherine sensed she was about to leave. Still speechless, Catherine watched her go. As Catherine got up, she saw the child again, who led her back to her room. All the lights were still on. Catherine later said that she knew the child was her guardian angel.

When she got back to her bed, she heard the clock strike. It was two o'clock in the morning. Catherine did not sleep for the rest of the night. She lay awake, pondering what she had seen and everything our Lady had said. Why had Mary chosen her? And how would Catherine be able to do all that Mary had asked of her?

7

A SPECIAL MISSION

Catherine jumped up as soon as the morning bell rang. She was still wide awake. It was the feast of Saint Vincent, an important day for the community. Yet Catherine could think of nothing else but her meeting with our Lady. She went over and over it in her mind, firmly committing all the details to memory.

Catherine knew she had to tell Father Aladel about it. She trusted his guidance. Gathering up all her courage, she told him everything that had happened.

But as Catherine spoke, Father Aladel shook his head in disbelief. "No, no," he told Catherine. "This can't be! Stop filling your head with such silly things. Holiness doesn't consist in visions, but in true faith. Jesus told us in the Gospel, 'Blessed are those who have not seen, but still believe.' I want you to stop thinking about all this."

"But Father," Catherine protested, "I really did see Mary! And she told me all those things that I've told you!"

The priest sighed. "Our Lady is pleased with obedience. Now I am asking you, in obedience, to put all these foolish thoughts aside."

Catherine felt deeply disappointed. She knew that she had really seen Mary, but she also knew that God wanted her to follow the advice of Father Aladel. So Catherine did as he asked. She went about her duties, prayed, and lovingly served the poor. Still, she felt troubled that Father Aladel did not believe her.

Toward the end of July, political troubles came to France. The king, Charles X, was overthrown, and another king put in his place. Mobs gathered and there was rioting in Paris. During these violent days, however, all the sisters were kept safe.

Father Aladel took notice. He began to wonder. Catherine had claimed Mary had said, "France will suffer hard times. The throne will be cast down." For it to happen so soon . . . could it just be a coincidence? Perhaps there *was* something to what Catherine had told him. He began to wonder, but he still didn't believe Catherine's tale.

Catherine tried her best to follow Father Aladel's instructions. She just kept on doing her work as usual. The summer turned to fall, and then the cold days of November arrived.

It was five thirty in the evening on Saturday, November 27, four months after Catherine's first vision of our Lady. The next day would be the first Sunday of Advent. Catherine was in chapel for the evening meditation. As she was praying, Catherine suddenly heard a familiar sound. She had heard it once before, when she first saw the Blessed Mother. It was the sound of the rustling of a silk dress.

Startled, Catherine looked up. Mary was there again! She was standing on the right side of the altar, near the picture of Saint Joseph. Catherine noticed that Mary's dress was white with plain sleeves, and that our Lady was wearing a blue mantle or cloak. She also had on a long veil, the pale yellow color of dawn. She held something in her hands. It looked like a large ball. She was holding it up, as if to offer it to God.

Then Catherine's eyes caught sight of something else. Mary was wearing beautiful rings on her fingers. They were made of exquisite gems, and brilliant light was streaming from them. These rays of light were like sunbeams, and were so bright that Catherine could not see Mary's feet.

Our Lady turned and looked at Catherine. Solemnly, she said, "This ball that you see represents the whole world, especially France, and each person in particular." Then, referring to the light coming from the gems, Mary said, "These rays symbolize the graces I obtain for all those who ask for them." But not all the rings on Mary's fingers gave light. Mary explained, "The gems from which rays do not fall symbolize the graces that people forget to ask for." Catherine realized how important it is to pray and to ask God for the graces we need.

As Catherine watched, the vision began to change. Mary no longer held the ball. Instead, she held out both hands, one at each side. The rays continued to stream from her fingers. Then Catherine saw the whole scene in an oval frame. Around the edges, words appeared: "O Mary, conceived without sin, pray for us who have recourse to thee."

Catherine understood that these words were a prayer to Mary. The prayer was in honor of Mary's great holiness and purity. It would help those who pray it entrust all their needs to Mary.

Catherine then heard Mary say, "Have a medal made with this image. All who wear it will receive great graces; they should wear it around the neck. Graces will abound for all those who wear it with confidence."

The image turned around. Catherine saw that on the back, the medal had a large letter *M*. Over it was a bar and a cross. Under it were two hearts: the hearts of Jesus and Mary. The heart of Jesus was crowned with thorns, and the heart of Mary was pierced with a sword. Twelve stars surrounded the whole image.

Then it was over.

Catherine felt peace and joy. In the afterglow of the vision, she finished her prayer, went to supper, and talked with the other sisters as usual. But she didn't say anything about what she had seen.

When she saw Father Aladel again, she told him about this new vision. *Oh, no!* the priest thought. *Not again!* Just as he had before, he told Catherine that it was all an illusion. "If you want to be like our Lady," he warned, "just do one thing: imitate her virtues. As for the rest, beware of your imagination!"

Turned away again, Catherine didn't know what to do. Our Lady had given her the mission of having this medal made. She had also told Catherine to tell her spiritual director about the visions. But Father Aladel thought Catherine had made the whole thing up. What could she do now?

BACK TO THE FARM

During the next month, December, Catherine saw the vision one more time. This time it also happened while Catherine was praying in chapel, at five thirty in the afternoon. Just like before, she heard the rustle of our Lady's silk dress. Mary appeared in the same way, with her hands stretched out. Brilliant rays of light streamed from them. Catherine heard a voice saying to her, "These rays of light symbolize the graces that our Lady obtains for those who ask for them."

The vision lasted for a long while. Then it gradually faded away. She later wrote, "It all slipped away from sight, like a candle being gently blown out." In her heart, Catherine heard the words, "You will no longer see me, but you will hear my voice when you pray." The young sister realized that this was the last time she would see the Blessed Mother. Still, Catherine felt happy and joyful. Mary was so beautiful! She was so loving! She was just like a tender mother, watching over her children.

But now Catherine had a problem. The Blessed Mother had given Catherine a special mission: to have a medal made with the image of our Lady as Catherine had seen her. Mary wanted it to be widely distributed. But so far, every time Catherine talked to Father Aladel, he refused to believe her.

Catherine tried once more but got the same answer. In prayer she told Mary, "You'd better appear to someone else, because Father doesn't believe me."

Catherine had told her spiritual director about the visions and the medal, just as Mary had asked, so now she just turned it over to Mary, trusting that somehow our Lady would make it work out.

On January 30, 1831, Catherine's novitiate ended. She received the habit of the Daughters of Charity, but did not yet make her vows. That would come later. For now, she still had more to learn, so she was sent to a place where she could start to work more with the poor.

On February 5, Catherine arrived at the Enghien (pronounced *AHN-ghee-yenh*) Hospice. It was in Reuilly (pronounced *ROO-yih*), a suburb of Paris, only a few miles from the motherhouse. At this hospice, the sisters took care of elderly and sick men and women, especially those who had worked for the king or served in the military. Catherine was assigned to work in the kitchen, helping the head cook, Sister Vincent. Catherine was used to this work from all her experience on her family's farm. She got into the work right away, helping to cook and serve the meals.

One day in the kitchen, as Catherine was preparing big helpings of food for the poor, Sister Vincent frowned. "Sister Catherine," she said, "what are you doing? You're using up too much food!"

Surprised, Catherine replied, "But the men are hungry. They have big appetites and need enough to eat!"

"But our supplies are limited," Sister Vincent said. "We have to conserve them." With that, she reached over and took away some of the food that Catherine had been preparing.

Catherine looked down at what was left. It didn't seem like there would be enough for everyone. So she just did her best with what she had.

This incident disturbed Catherine. She felt that the people were not getting enough food. Some of the men even asked if they could have more. Sadly, Catherine shook her head. "That's all we have," was all she could say.

Then she remembered something Saint Vincent often said, "Love is inventive." He meant that love finds ways to meet the people's needs. Catherine had an idea.

A large garden surrounded the hospice. With all her experience from the farm, Catherine knew she could make the land more productive. She got permission to take over the garden. Under her expert care, the large garden turned into a real farm. Catherine improved the farming methods so that the land produced more food. She nurtured the hens in the henhouse, and every morning she came away with a large basket of eggs. Soon, the pantry was overflowing with food. Catherine smiled when the men asked her if they could have more. "Yes, of course!" she said, as she gave them second helpings of soup, vegetables, eggs, and bread.

This work on the farm and in the kitchen took all of Catherine's time and energy. For now she could do nothing about the mission of the medal that the Blessed Mother had given her. But she didn't forget about it. In prayer, she asked Mary, "How am I to go about this? If you really want this medal, show me what to do to make it happen!"

9

THE MEDAL

Catherine no longer saw our Lady, but in prayer, she continued to receive some gentle promptings. A voice she heard inside her heart urged her to act. One day in the spring of 1831, Catherine saw Father Aladel and began to walk toward him. He knew what she was going to say, so he told her right away, "You have to put all those illusions out of your mind! Don't speak to me about them! I don't want to hear it."

Catherine was disappointed, but not surprised. At least she had made the effort.

The summer passed quickly. Catherine was busy on the farm at the hospice, but she kept hearing the inner voice. It wouldn't let the matter rest. In prayer, Catherine protested to Mary, "But Father Aladel won't listen to me!"

Then Catherine heard these words in her heart, "He is my servant. He should be afraid of displeasing me!"

So that fall, Catherine went to see Father Aladel again. Just like before, he told her to stop imagining things. But this time Catherine had the courage to tell him, "The Blessed Virgin is angry!"

Father Aladel sent Catherine on her way. He gave no sign of what he was thinking. But in reality, Catherine's words had shaken him. *This young sister is so determined,* he thought. *What if she really* did *see the Blessed Virgin? And what if our Lady really is not pleased with me for doubting?*

So the priest thought about it more, and prayed more deeply over the matter. He decided to ask for some advice and sought out a priest friend of his, Father Étienne (pronounced *AY-tee-en*).

"There is a young Daughter of Charity who comes to me for spiritual direction. She claims to have seen the Blessed Virgin."

Father Étienne replied, "Do you think she is just making it up?"

Father Aladel paused. "The odd thing about it is that this sister is not the type of person who dreams up visions. She comes from a farm. She is hard-working and has a level head. She is the last person I would have thought would have a vision. But I just couldn't believe it. So I told her to stop telling me about it."

"But she keeps on coming back to you?" Father Étienne asked.

"Yes," Father Aladel said. "And that's not all. She claims that our Lady wants her to have a medal struck. It is to be patterned on the vision that she saw. The last time I spoke to this sister, she told me that the Blessed Virgin is angry!"

"Angry!" Father Étienne gasped. "At you?"

"Yes," Father Aladel sighed. "That's when I began to have my doubts. What if this sister really did see our Lady? How can I be an obstacle to what the Blessed Virgin is asking?"

"I have an idea," Father Étienne said. "Why don't we go to the Superior General, Father Salhorgne (pronounced *sal-ORN-yuh*), and tell him about this? Then if you follow his advice, at least you can say you are acting in obedience."

Father Aladel was relieved. "That's a good idea! Let's do it!"

So the two priests went to see their superior. Much to Father Aladel's surprise, Father Salhorgne was in favor of the idea of making a medal. He made a suggestion. "I have a meeting scheduled soon to see Archbishop

Quélen (pronounced *KAY-lahn*), the archbishop of Paris," he told them. "Why don't you come along with me? It's a good opportunity to ask him about it."

They agreed and went to see the archbishop.

During the meeting Father Aladel explained what Catherine had said about the apparition, and especially about the medal. The priest was worried that the archbishop would think it was all foolishness. But to his surprise, the archbishop liked the idea! He especially liked the way that Mary was portrayed as obtaining graces. He thought it would be a beautiful expression of faith.

"I don't see any problem with making this medal," the archbishop said. "It doesn't mean that we have to say the apparition was real or not. All we will do is distribute the medal. Then later we can judge the tree by its fruits."

Father Aladel felt like a great weight had been lifted from him. Now he could be at peace. Surely our Lady would be pleased with him! Now that the way was clear, he lost no time. He drew up a design of the image just as Catherine had described it to him.

He also spoke with Catherine about it. She was overjoyed to hear that the archbishop had given permission for the medal. She was at peace, knowing that the mission our Lady had given her was beginning to be fulfilled.

Father Aladel asked her, "What about the design on the back of the medal? Was there an inscription around it, like on the front?"

Catherine told him that she didn't remember exactly. But she would pray about it. Soon she came back and told him she had heard our Lady's voice in her heart, saying, "The 'M' and the two hearts on the back of the medal will be enough."

10

MIRACLES

Catherine was anxious for the medal to be made. Father Aladel had contacted a jeweler to inquire about producing it. But suddenly, toward the end of March 1832, disaster struck. An epidemic of cholera broke out in Paris. Cholera is a terrible disease and many people got sick and died.

The hospitals couldn't cope with all the sick people, so Father Étienne opened some of the priests' buildings to help care for them. Father Aladel was also very busy taking care of the sick people. He went everywhere he could, giving the last sacraments to people and praying with them.

In the midst of all this, he couldn't pursue the project of making the medals. But by the end of May, the worst of the epidemic was over, and things began to get back to normal.

Father Aladel completed the final arrangements for the medals. The first one thousand, five hundred of them were delivered on June 30.

In early July, the medals were distributed to the Daughters of Charity as well. Both Catherine and Father Aladel kept the secret about the apparitions. So the other sisters did not know that Catherine was the one behind the medals. When the other sisters stepped up to get their medals, Catherine did, too. One sister said to her, "I wonder how these medals came to be? Do you think our Lady revealed herself to one of us?"

Catherine replied, "If she did, it would have been a most beautiful grace." She kept her secret well! The only other thing she said was, "Now the medal must be distributed to everyone."

The sisters helped with this task. As they went about visiting the sick, they offered people the medal. Catherine made special efforts to help with this task. She wanted everyone to pray to our Lady and ask for the graces that God wants to give them through Mary. One day Catherine was visiting with one of the elderly ladies at the hospice. She offered a medal to the woman, saying, "Would you like to have one of these new medals of our Lady?"

"What new medal?" the woman said.

Catherine explained, "The medal has been made because our Blessed Mother

"I wonder how these medals came to be? Do you think our Lady revealed herself to one of us?"

asked for it. It shows Mary with her hands outstretched, with rays of light coming from them. The rays of light represent the graces she wants to obtain for us from God."

"Yes, I would like one!" the woman replied. "I've been sick for so long. Maybe the medal will make me better."

Catherine explained to her, "Remember that the medal isn't a good luck charm. It's an expression of faith. It reminds us that when we pray and ask Mary to help us, she prays for us to God. There is a prayer engraved on the medal, 'O Mary, conceived without sin, pray for us who have recourse to thee.'"

"I understand," the woman said. "I know that Mary cares about me and will obtain graces for me."

"That's right," Catherine said. "Our faith and trust in God is the most important thing. When you look at the medal, it will remind you to turn to Mary with great trust."

Catherine and the other sisters continued to give the medals out freely. Then they started to hear stories about people who had been helped by it. People began to report cures. A teenage boy who had been bitten by a dog became very sick, probably with rabies. The sisters prayed and gave him a medal, and he was completely cured. Then there was the case of a young woman who was expecting a baby. She developed some serious health problems and was in danger of losing the child. She obtained a medal, and she and her family began to pray for a good outcome. She got better and delivered a healthy baby.

But that wasn't all. Conversions were being reported, too. An old soldier who was at the point of dying was full of anger and bitterness. He even cursed God. A sister spoke to him with gentleness and care, and she persuaded him to accept a medal. His heart softened and he turned to God and confessed his sins. He even said to the sister, "It pains me that I have come to love God so late in life, and that my love is so small!" Then he died a holy death.

Besides these, many other cases of people being cured and others being converted were reported. The spread of the medal was giving rise to a great spirit of religious fervor. People were returning to the Church and receiving the sacraments again. These things were so sudden and unexpected that people started to say the medal was *miraculous!* Little by little, the expression became popular. That's how the *miraculous medal* got its name. The medal itself was not working miracles, because it can't. God was looking at the faith of the people using it. The medal was like kindling used to start a fire. It brought about something bigger than itself: the fire of God's love in people's hearts.

But with its success, people began to ask where it came from. Where did this miraculous medal originate? How could it be explained in a way that would protect Catherine's secret?

11

Catherine's Secret

One of the priests who helped the bishop was named Abbé Le Guillou (pronounced *ah-BAY luh GEE-you*). He came up with a good idea that would tell people something about the story of the medal. At the same time, it would keep Catherine's secret.

He would write a booklet called *Mary's Month*. Booklets like these were popular at the time. So the Abbé asked Father Aladel to write down the story of what happened, but without giving too many details. Father Aladel did not mention Catherine's name. He just said that someone had seen the vision. The booklet was printed in April 1834 and was a great success. Thousands of copies sold right away.

But people asked for more information. So then Father Aladel wrote more about the medal. This time, the booklet gave a little more information. It did not identify Catherine by name, but it did say that the person who saw Mary was a novice in Paris, in one of the communities that serve the poor. Father Aladel asked Catherine's permission to put these details in the booklet, and she gave it. Over sixty thousand copies of the booklet were printed before the end of the year.

The medal was also being spread far and wide. It went to many other countries outside France, including the United States, China, and Russia. By 1839, more than ten million medals had been distributed all over the world!

As the medal spread, people began to wonder about the vision it was based on. But Catherine kept her secret. It would have been easy for her to go public with it and get a lot of attention. But that was not her way. She didn't want fame for herself. Whenever anybody tried to guess or ask her about the vision, she always answered in a clever way that kept her identity hidden.

Catherine was still working in the hospice at Enghien. She was now taking care of the laundry. She would not only wash and iron the clothes, but would also mend and patch them when they had holes.

One day the superior said to Catherine, "I've been thinking that you might like to do more than just laundry."

"What do you have in mind?" Catherine asked.

"We could use more sisters to help take care of the elderly men. It can be hard work. As you know, some of the men are gruff and may use bad language. They can be bad tempered and difficult to deal with."

"I can handle it," Catherine said.

"Yes," the superior said, "I think you can. You come from a hard-working background and know how to manage people."

"On my family's farm, I supervised the farmhands. I knew how to get their respect," Catherine replied. "I will be happy to work with the people here."

So Catherine started this new task. She brought to it her usual strength and skill.

But Catherine was also preparing for another important event. On May 3, 1835, she made her first profession of religious vows. In general, religious sisters take three vows: chastity, poverty, and obedience. But as a Daughter of Charity, Catherine took a special fourth vow that Saint Vincent had given them. It was a vow to serve persons who were poor, sick, and in need. Catherine would renew these vows every year.

Catherine had been preparing for this for five years. As she made her vows at Mass that day, she prayed to Jesus to give her the strength to live them. Catherine felt so happy to give her life to the Lord and to serve the poor.

12

ORDINARY LIFE

Between caring for the elderly men and working on the farm, Catherine lived a busy life! Under her direction, the farm flourished. She knew how to manage the land and the animals—except for the cows.

In 1846, Catherine decided it would be a good idea to get some cows. So she bought her first cow. It soon got sick and she had to sell it at a loss. But Catherine kept on trying. Over sixteen years, she bought and sold thirty different cows! She was happy because she had fresh milk to give to the people at the hospice. But Catherine wasn't very good at selling them for a reasonable price.

In 1860, a new superior came to the Enghien hospice. Her name was Sister Dufès (pronounced *DOO-feh*). After a while she asked Catherine, "How are things going with the cows? Are we losing money by keeping them?"

Catherine told her, "I have kept a careful record of all the times I have bought and sold cows. Also, I have kept a record of how much milk they have given. Let me show you."

So Catherine got out her record book and showed it to Sister Dufès, who studied it carefully. Then she said, "Sister Catherine, you have certainly kept very good records. But the bottom line is that over the years we have lost 3,655 gold francs in buying and selling cows! How is that possible?" (That much money at Catherine's time equals about seventeen thousand dollars today!)

Catherine thought this over. "Well, my father taught me many things about farming, but he never taught me how to buy and sell cows. Sometimes the poor cows are not in very good condition when I sell them. I don't want to overcharge the buyers. But don't forget about all the milk that they've given. The people here like it so much!"

Sister Dufès sighed. "I know how much this means to you, Sister Catherine, but we're losing too much money on these cows. You have to stop right away."

Catherine was disappointed that she could no longer provide fresh milk. But she obeyed and stopped the work with the cows. However, the farm still had other animals that she took care of very well: the chickens, the doves, and even a few horses.

She liked working on the farm because it enabled her to provide fresh food for all the residents at the hospice. The other sisters knew that if Catherine was collecting food, she would always give the best of it to the elderly people.

The men were often gruff and irritable with the sisters. Sometimes they said mean and hurtful things! But Catherine was always gentle and patient with them.

One day a sister said to her, "Sister Catherine, you are too lenient with the men. You have to be much stricter with them."

But Catherine said only, "I see Christ in them. I can't treat them harshly." And that was the end of it.

Another day Catherine was taking a turn answering the door. The doorbell rang. Catherine put aside her knitting and got up to answer the door. She instantly recognized the woman standing there.

"Blaisine (pronounced *blay-ZEEN*)!" Catherine greeted her warmly. Blaisine was middle-aged. She wore an old dress, with several patches and dirty spots. She held a bag that seemed to contain all her possessions. When she smiled, she revealed several missing teeth. Catherine knew Blaisine from many years before. She had a difficult personality. She often became stressed or angry and would yell and scream at others. But now she was happy to see Catherine.

"Sister Catherine," she said, "how well I remember you!"

"Yes, Blaisine," Catherine said, "I remember you too! What have you been doing?"

"Well, Sister Catherine," the woman responded, "I've gotten along. But truthfully, not too well. Lately I've taken to wandering around the streets begging for food. Most people just look the other way."

Catherine nodded and ushered her in. "Sit down here and wait a moment. I will get you something hot to drink and a bit of food."

While Blaisine waited, Catherine went to talk to the superior. She explained the situation and got permission to take Blaisine into the hospice. The sisters would take care of her, since she couldn't take care of herself.

Catherine always treated her well. Blaisine still became angry and emotional frequently and was difficult to live with. But Catherine handled this with tact and charity. Blaisine too was one of the poor. Saint Vincent had often told the sisters, "You are servants of the poor." Catherine took those words to heart.

13

FIRE!

Catherine welcomed everyone, including the young women who entered the community wanting to become sisters. She was always there, among the first to greet them. She gave them a warm welcome and tried to make them feel at home.

Sometimes they got homesick. Catherine wanted to help these young women follow their call from God.

One day Catherine was outside in the garden. There she met a young sister, who had recently been sent to Enghien. The sister seemed downcast. Catherine asked gently, "Something is bothering you, isn't it?"

Sister Fouquet (pronounced *FOO-kay*) replied, "I entered the community in order to care for the sick. I can't speak in front of groups of people!"

Catherine asked, "What do you mean?"

"I was sent to Boulogne (pronounced *BOO-luhn-yuh*), to take care of the children. I love doing that. One of my duties was to teach them catechism. The children were no problem. But the classes were open to anyone, and their parents started to stay as well. I felt embarrassed to speak before these adults! I don't know enough to teach them. Now I'm thinking that I should just go back to my family."

"Oh, I see," Catherine replied. "Don't be afraid! I'll pray to Mary for you. Promise me that for the next year, you will do the same. You'll see! You will study well and pass your tests. You will find happiness in your vocation!"

And it worked out just like Catherine had said. In the end, Sister Fouquet became a happy Daughter of Charity. She was even sent to take care of sick, elderly people, something she had always wanted to do.

Catherine kept up with her work at the hospice. There were other needs, though. At that time, many children were forced to work in factories. Some of these children were orphans. They lived in bad conditions, or they ended up in the street with no place to live. The sisters ran a boarding school for the orphans. They taught the children basic skills, and they prepared them for their first Holy Communion.

The conditions in the factories where the children worked were unsafe. One of these buildings was a wallpaper factory. It was located right next to the sisters' house. On February 17, 1863, a fire broke out in the factory. It spread quickly, sweeping through the wooden building.

Sister Philomene (pronounced *FEEL-oh-min*) ran to tell the superior, "Sister Dufès, come quickly! A fire is burning the factory down! It's right next to the chapel and the flames are already licking our roof!"

Sister Dufès and the other sisters went outside. Terrified, they looked on as the fire grew and spread.

"Hurry!" Sister Dufès said. "Get everyone out of the building!"

But one person stayed calm: Catherine. She said to Sister Dufès and all the sisters, "Don't get scared! The fire will stop and no one will be harmed!" Then Catherine went over to the statue of the Blessed Mother that was in the garden and began to pray. The other sisters watched, horrified as the flames seemed to leap higher. But then, Sister Philomene cried out, "Look! The flames are

*"Don't get scared! The fire will stop
and no one will be harmed!"*

dying down!" It was true. Amazingly, the flames began to die out. The factory was burned down, but the sisters' house and the residents were safe. The Blessed Mother had protected them.

14

ANOTHER MISSION FOR FATHER ALADEL

"Did you hear about the new group that Father Aladel is directing?" one of the sisters asked at breakfast.

"What group is that?" said Catherine.

"Seven years ago, a sixteen-year-old girl named Bénigne Hairon (pronounced *BAY-neen-yuh AIR-on*) started an organization called the Children of Mary. That was in 1838. Now it has spread throughout France and has come to Paris, and Father Étienne asked Father Aladel to direct it."

Just as Mary said it would be, Catherine thought, and smiled to herself.

Back in 1830, Mary had given Catherine another task in addition to having the medal made. Not long after the vision about the medal, Catherine went to talk to Father Aladel. She had something else to tell him, something that the Blessed Mother wanted him to know. Catherine braced herself before talking to him. She knew from experience that Father Aladel did not like to hear about these messages.

"Father Aladel," Catherine began, "I have something important to tell you."

The priest groaned to himself. *Oh no, here we go again,* he thought.

Aloud he asked, "What is it, Sister Catherine?"

"The Blessed Mother has another task for you. She wants you to establish a society to honor her. And she wants you to direct it. The name of this group will be the Association of the Children of Mary. Our Lady will obtain many graces for this group. She wants it to celebrate the month of May in her honor."

Father Aladel was not happy with this request. *How can I really know for sure that this sister has seen the Blessed Mother? What if Catherine just dreamed it all up?*

"Catherine, I've already told you that you need to forget all this talk of visions."

"But Father," Catherine protested, "Mary has told me she wants this! How can I tell her no?"

He replied, "If this request is really coming from our Lady, she will find a way to make it happen."

Catherine gathered up her courage and tried once more. "She wants to make it happen through *you*, Father. You will have to find a way to obey her."

Catherine left. She was again frustrated at Father Aladel's lack of belief, so she went to chapel and prayed, "Oh Mary, if you want this to happen, you have to convince Father Aladel! He does not believe me!"

In her heart, Catherine felt that the Blessed Mother was telling her it would all come true in due time.

Fifteen years later, in 1845, it did. The group wasn't started by Father Aladel. But by that time, Father Aladel took on the task willingly.

It became an association approved by the Pope. The Daughters of Charity spread the movement through their schools. And through it, they distributed the miraculous medal far and wide.

On the farm at Enghien, Catherine was always happy to bring in the food she harvested, because she knew how much the men loved to eat. She wanted them to have plenty of food. And they loved her for it. One evening, one of the men waited until the end of their meal. He got up and said, "Please, quiet down, everyone! I have something important to say."

Little by little the men's voices died down, and the clatter of silverware ended.

The man looked directly at Catherine and said, "Sister, we are so grateful for all that you do for us! Whenever you serve our meals, you always ask, 'Are you sure you've had enough?' Thank you for your generosity and kindness!"

Catherine blushed and thanked him. She said, "Saint Vincent always said that God's providence will never fail us when we are generous to others!" Then she hurried off to the kitchen, not wanting to draw more attention to herself.

In fact, Catherine always faced the challenge of not drawing attention to herself. After the story of the medal had been made public, people wanted to know which sister had seen the Blessed Mother. Although Catherine always kept her secret, other people started to speculate. They knew it was a sister in a congregation that served the poor, who had been a novice in 1830. So that narrowed down the possibilities.

*"Sister, we are so grateful
for all that you do for us!"*

Some of the sisters did suspect that Catherine was the visionary. And sometimes they would try to trick her into revealing herself. In 1855, a sister named Sister Charvier (pronounced *SHAR-vee-ay*) came to Enghien. She had heard some rumors that Catherine was the visionary and decided to try to figure it out. She later testified, "I got the idea that maybe it had been Sister Catherine who saw Mary. So I paid close attention to her. She was very prayerful and humble, but I didn't think she was the visionary. She didn't seem like a mystic."

But the idea kept coming back to her. One day she happened to be in the same room as Catherine. She saw a statue of our Lady on a mantelpiece. Sister Charvier asked, "Sister Catherine, was that what the Blessed Virgin looked like when you saw her?"

But Catherine was too wise to fall into such a trap. "Go along now, and mind your own business!" she replied.

Most people didn't even suspect it was Catherine who had seen our Lady. Catherine was too humble, too hidden, too out of the way. She quietly did all the hardest work. Whether it was harvesting the vegetables, waxing the floors, or feeding the elderly people, she blended into the background.

However, Catherine's superior, Sister Dufès, did know her secret. The information had been given to her confidentially when she became superior. She carefully guarded Catherine's secret too. But one day, some people who had helped the community told the superior that they would like to see the visionary. At first, Sister Dufès refused, as she always did. But they insisted. They began to feel offended. Because these people were good friends of the sisters, Sister Dufès reluctantly decided to allow it. "All right," she said. "Let's go to the dining room where the elderly people eat. That is where the sister is usually found."

But they had hardly come in when Catherine noticed them. She realized what they were up to, and she slipped outside until they were gone!

15

THE WAR

Two events shook Catherine's busy and quiet life at Enghien. In 1865, Father Aladel suddenly suffered a massive stroke and died. Catherine was saddened when she heard this news, but she was confident that our Lady would take this good priest to heaven. He had been a faithful friend to her and had done much to promote the miraculous medal and the Children of Mary.

Five years later, in July 1870, the French emperor declared war on Prussia (an area that now includes parts of Poland, Russia, Germany, and other countries in central and eastern Europe). Catherine was sixty-four years old.

The sisters began to pray when they heard about the war. Catherine said, "The poor soldiers!" thinking of those who would be killed and wounded.

The war did not go well for the French forces. The Prussians had a stronger army and swept through the countryside. Soon, they were advancing on Paris and laid siege to the city. The sisters were afraid, not only for themselves but for all the poor people they were taking care of.

More people came to them seeking food and help. By September, the sisters were feeding about twelve hundred people every day! The work was very hard and it was difficult to calm the people. Most of them were anxious and upset. The sisters too were worried.

Catherine tried to encourage them. "Don't be afraid! Our Lady will take care of us as she always has."

"But what should we do if the war comes closer and we can't get food for the elderly people?" another sister asked.

"Let's pray all the more. We can put some miraculous medals around the building, on the windows and the doors. Put them right in the middle of the front door!"

The Prussians won the war, and the French government collapsed. By March 1871, civil disorder was spreading in Paris.

Besides taking care of the elderly and the sick, the sisters were also looking after about 200 wounded soldiers in their hospice at Enghien. In April, on Good Friday, some trouble started. A rumor began that two of the men in the hospice had committed crimes. Some people wanted to take them and shoot them. A crowd gathered outside the door of the sisters' medical building.

"Let us in! Give us the men! We demand they be punished!"

"But why? These men haven't done anything!" Sister Dufès protested.

More people started to arrive. The din and confusion got worse. The two wounded men could not escape, so they were brought to the guardhouse in town where some soldiers were staying. Sister Dufès ran there and begged for their release.

"Please help us!" she shouted. "The crowd wants to kill these two men! But they haven't done anything wrong! They didn't hurt anyone!" She continued to beg.

Finally, the soldiers went out and quieted the crowd. The two innocent men were allowed to go back to the hospital until they recovered.

For now, no harm had come to anyone. But the days were growing darker.

Because of all the trouble, the priests hadn't been able to come to the sisters' house to celebrate Mass. But on Easter

Sunday, one of the priests managed to get through. Catherine was so happy to be able to attend Mass, especially for Easter!

But that night, trouble started again. The crowd that had come on Friday seeking the two men came back. They would not be satisfied until they had them. They broke into the house. "Give us those two men!" they shouted.

Sister Dufès remained strong and fearless. "We will never give them to you! They have done nothing wrong!"

The leader of the group swore at her. Then he said, "We will search until we find them!"

They went through the hospice. But the men were hiding and could not be found.

Still angry, the leader demanded, "Since we can't find the men, we will take Sister Dufès with us!" A look of fear crossed her face. But she remained calm. Then some of the sick soldiers came and stood behind her. After that, all of the sisters gathered around Sister Dufès. "You'll have to take us too!" they told the leader of the mob.

He backed down. The crowd left. The sisters were safe—for now.

16

MORE TROUBLE

The new informal government, called the Commune, was unfriendly toward the Church and the sisters. They were angry that Sister Dufès had not let them get the two men they wanted. Soon after, they issued a warrant for her arrest. The charge was "conspiracy." But some friends of the sisters heard about it, and she was able to go into hiding in the city of Versailles (pronounced *ver-SIGH*), where things were safer.

With the superior gone, Catherine took charge of the situation. Above all, she wanted to make sure that the sisters and the people at the hospice would be safe. In order to prevent trouble and explain the sisters' situation, she went to see the rebels at their headquarters.

She walked in. The rebels were surprised to see her. "What are you doing here?" one asked.

"I am here to explain that Sister Dufès has done nothing wrong. Why have you issued an arrest warrant for her?"

"She hid the two men we wanted to arrest!" one of the men said.

About fifty men were there, some standing around, others sitting at a table. Some of them even had guns. Catherine knew she was in a dangerous place, but she trusted that Mary would protect her.

One of the younger men started to shout at her and call her names. Soon the others joined in. Catherine's face flashed with anger, but she stood her ground. After the yelling and shouting died down a bit, she said with great courage, "Let me explain."

She explained that Sister Duffy was only protecting the men who had come to the sisters for help.

One man shouted, "Lies! You are lying! And if it is true, you should have told us before!"

Catherine replied, "It's not our job to be the police. Besides, the two men had official documents!"

Angrily, another man shouted, "Let's arrest her!"

Undaunted, Catherine said, "You can't arrest me without a warrant! Show me your documents!"

At that, one man took his sword and held it up to Catherine. "This is my warrant!" he threatened.

Several of the men started to surround her, ready to drag her away to jail. But one of the men there had been taken care of by the sisters when he was sick. He didn't want to see Catherine get arrested. So he stepped in, took Catherine by both arms, and dragged her out to safety. Catherine was shaken but unhurt.

The people running the government wanted to get people to stop practicing their religion. They looked for ways to stop the sisters from teaching people about God. It was difficult for them to do this, because the people loved and supported the sisters who took such good care of the sick and the poor.

One day, two women from the government came to Enghien. They went straight to Sister Angélique Tanguy (pronounced *TAHN-ghee*), who was now taking Sister Dufès's place, and said, "We're here to replace the sisters!"

Sister Tanguy was shocked. "What!" she said. "How can that be? You can't just come in here and take over!"

"Here is the document that says we can," the women said, showing it to her.

Sister Tanguy read it. It said that there should be no more teaching about God, no more catechism classes, and no more crucifixes on the walls.

"We can't let you do this!" the sister protested. The two women backed down a little.

They shrugged and said, "We will come back." Then they left.

They did come back a few days later, with more women. One of the women actually went into a classroom and took over the class. They barged right in and wouldn't leave. But they couldn't make the sisters leave, either. The situation grew more tense as the days went by.

One day toward the end of April, Catherine heard some shouts. "What's going on?" one of the men asked her.

"I don't know," Catherine said, "but I'll find out."

She hurried out, only to find Sister Tanguy. She told Catherine, "Tell all the sisters to go upstairs and hide in the linen room. A group of men have broken in!"

The men had guns and were looking for things to steal. The sisters could hear their shouts from the room where they were hiding. One of the sisters said, "What if they go to chapel and take the Blessed Sacrament! I will go and get it!"

She managed to go to the chapel and bring the Blessed Sacrament back safely. As they waited in fear, the sisters lit two candles on a small table with the ciborium. They prayed in silent adoration.

Catherine reassured them that our Lady would take care of them and protect them from harm. Meanwhile, the men found some bottles of wine in the cellar. They drank it all and became drunk. Then they fell asleep.

The sisters knew it wasn't safe to stay there. In the middle of the night, while the men were still sleeping, the sisters slipped out of the linen room. They got a few necessary things and left the house.

Before leaving, Catherine stopped before the statue of Mary outside. The other sisters gathered around her, and they prayed for safety and guidance. It was April 30.

Catherine comforted the other sisters. She said, "We will be back here by the end of May!" Her calmness and serenity helped the other sisters who were more fearful. "We will be safe; nothing bad will happen to us!" Catherine said. And they hurried to safety.

17

INTO FLIGHT

Catherine and the other sisters went to one of their houses at Saint Denis (pronounced *sahn deh-NEE*), not too far from Paris. The superior of the community, Sister Randier (pronounced *RAHN-dee-ay*), gave them a warm welcome. "Sisters, it is so good to see you! Tell me what is happening in Paris!"

The sisters told her all about what had happened and how they had to flee from Enghien.

Then Sister Randier said, "I'm afraid I have some bad news. The local officials will only allow one of you to stay here. The rest will have to find refuge somewhere else."

Those who had families in the area went to stay with them until the trouble died down. The others went on to other community houses. By the next day, only Catherine and one other sister were left, Sister Tranchemere (pronounced *transh-MAIR*). They were good friends, as they had often worked together taking care of the elderly.

At this time, Catherine was sixty-five years old. Though she worked as hard as ever, she had some health problems, so she asked Sister Tranchemere to be her companion. Since they couldn't both stay at Saint Denis, they went together to another house at Ballainvilliers (pronounced *bah-YAHN-vee-yay*). Some of the old women from the Enghien hospice had been sent there. Catherine was very happy to see them. It was almost like being home.

In the meantime, Sister Dufès was still away. Catherine wrote her a letter saying that the whole community would return to Enghien by the end of May. It seemed impossible. But Catherine had great trust that Mary would intercede to protect them all and bring them back home.

However, things were getting worse in Paris. "Catherine, did you hear the news from Paris?" a sister asked her one day.

"No, what's happened?" she replied.

"Crowds have been rioting in the streets! They went into the church of Our Lady of Victories and sacked it! They stole the sacred vessels and destroyed the statues."

Catherine grew very serious. She knew that the church was the headquarters of an association connected with the miraculous medal. "They have attacked our Lady," she said. Then in a low tone she added, "They will not go farther."

Other troops went to Paris to fight the local rebels. The rebels took the archbishop of Paris hostage, along with other priests. On May 24, they shot and killed the archbishop and about twenty priests.

In late May, fighting spread and many fires broke out in Paris. Catherine heard about this, but she had complete trust that the Blessed Mother would indeed protect the sisters' house in Paris. Another sister, worried, asked, "What will happen to the motherhouse?"

Catherine said, completely at peace, "Don't worry about our houses. The Blessed Mother is watching over them. They will be safe!"

Anxiety and worry continued for a few more days. But then suddenly it was over. The army had conquered the rebels in Paris, and peace was established on May 28. Things began to calm down. The community could begin to reestablish itself.

On May 31, Sister Catherine, Sister Tranchemere, and Sister Dufès returned to Enghien. The other sisters who had scattered to various places also came back. It was the end of May and the community was reunited—just as Catherine had said! They found that Mary's statue in the garden had been damaged, but the house had survived intact, with no serious damage at all. Our Lady had indeed protected them.

18

BACK TO NORMAL

Catherine returned to her duties right away. Despite the chaos they had been through, things soon returned to normal. The elderly people who had been scattered gradually came back to the hospice. They were very happy to see Catherine, for she was their favorite. "Sister Catherine," one old woman said to her, "God is so good to allow me to come back here and see you again!"

But not everyone realized how holy Catherine was. In fact, some of the sisters took her for granted and even looked down on her at times. Catherine always kept the hardest tasks for herself. She would wax the floors of the hospice with a very heavy polishing machine. It was difficult to operate, but she kept on doing it even though she was getting older.

Sometimes young women who had just entered the Daughters of Charity, called postulants, were sent to the hospice to get used to religious life. In the spring of 1872, two young women, Gabrielle and Marie, joined the sisters at the hospice. One day when Gabrielle was out visiting her family, Catherine saw Marie. "How are you, Marie?" she asked. "Is something wrong? You look a little sad."

"Nothing is really wrong," Marie said. "I suppose I just feel a little homesick. I miss my family."

"Well, would you like to go with me on an outing?" Catherine asked her. "Have you ever seen our motherhouse on Rue du Bac?"

"No," Marie told her. "I would love to go there. I've heard that is where our Lady revealed the miraculous medal."

Catherine never gave away her secret. But she took Marie to the motherhouse and explained the story of the medal. In this way, Catherine helped Marie with her homesickness, and taught her about the medal at the same time.

Catherine's love for the poor never stopped growing. One day a woman came knocking on the door of the hospice. Catherine greeted her.

"Sister, can you help me please?" the woman began.

"What is it that you need?" Catherine asked her.

"I can't pay my rent. I need sixty francs. If I can't pay it soon, I will be evicted and I have no place to go!"

Catherine looked at the woman with great compassion. She thought of what Saint Vincent had often said, "You are servants of the poor!"

Catherine said to the woman, "Right now I don't have any money to give you. We have run out of funds too. But maybe I will be able to find someone who can help. Come back in a few days."

The woman left. A couple of days later, a wealthy woman who was a friend of the sisters came to visit. She often helped them with special needs. Catherine told her about the poor woman who couldn't pay her rent. The wealthy woman gave her the money.

When the poor woman came back a few days later, Catherine told her, "Here is the money for your rent! Pray for a generous woman who was willing to help."

"Thank you, Sister! How can I ever repay you?" the woman cried.

"When you have the opportunity, help someone else in turn," Catherine replied.

Helping people like this always gave Catherine great joy. She thought, *Saint Vincent said that we should always work with love to serve the poor, especially those who are most needy among them. Lord, help me to serve them as you would!*

So the days went by and Catherine continued this work that she loved. But something was bothering her. It was connected to the apparitions of our Lady. Mary had wanted something else that still needed to be done. But first, Catherine had to face another difficulty.

19

SOME CHANGES

Catherine had been in charge of the farm and the hospice for a long time. She enjoyed taking care of the elderly people. And she knew how to run the hospice, the farm, and the kitchen very well.

One day in 1874, Sister Dufès called Catherine aside. "Sister Catherine, I have come to a decision. Things are changing a bit and I have decided to put Sister Tanguy in charge of the hospice. You will still do your work. But she will be the one making all the decisions."

Catherine felt let down. She liked her work at the hospice. Sister Tanguy was much younger, only thirty-six years old. She was a good sister, but Catherine wondered if she would change the way things were done. Catherine, in her sixties, felt like she was being put aside, but she was always obedient. "I accept your decision, Sister Dufès," she told her superior. "I will fully cooperate with Sister Tanguy."

Some of the other sisters appreciated Catherine's experience, and thought that she should still be in charge. One of Catherine's tasks each night was to go through the hospice and make sure all the doors were locked. She had a big ring with a lot of keys on it. Holding the keys was a symbol of her authority. Some of the sisters said to Catherine, "Hold on to the keys. Don't give them up!"

But Catherine would have none of that. "Tonight I will give them to Sister Tanguy, because she is the one in charge now." And she did exactly that. What mattered most to Catherine was serving the poor. She did have her own ways of doing things, and sometimes it was hard for her to give them up and follow Sister Tanguy's way, but Catherine was determined to do this with a generous and willing heart. She saw God's will in the situation and that was enough for her.

So Catherine continued her humble and quiet service of God's poor. It didn't matter to her that she was no longer in charge. All that mattered was seeing Christ in the poor and serving them.

Catherine knew that she was drawing near to the end of her life. She had carried out the task of the miraculous medal that our Lady had given to her. But Mary had made two other requests, both of which Catherine had not succeeded in fulfilling. With this in mind, one day in May 1876 she approached Sister Dufès and said, "I need to talk to you."

"Very well, Sister Catherine," Sister Dufès replied.

"But first I have to ask the Blessed Mother's advice. I will pray to her and see what she tells me to say. I will let you know tomorrow morning."

The next morning, Catherine said to Sister Dufès, "I am ready now to tell you everything." Wide-eyed, Sister Dufès ushered Catherine into her office.

Catherine usually did not talk very much. But now she began to talk and she did not stop for two hours! She told Sister Dufès all about the apparitions. First she explained the apparitions of the heart of Saint Vincent. Then she explained what had happened during the visions concerning the miraculous medal.

Sister Dufès was overwhelmed to hear Catherine describe all this. "Sister Catherine, as superior, I knew that you were the sister who received the visions about the miraculous medal, but I never spoke to you about it. I knew you wanted it to be a secret."

"Yes, I did," Catherine replied. "But there is one more thing that has to be done. Besides the medal, our Lady wanted a statue made of her holding a globe. The globe represents all the people in the world. Our Lady held it in her hands, showing how much she loves everyone on the earth. She wants them all to be close to her son Jesus."

"But Sister Catherine," Sister Dufès objected, "didn't you tell Father Aladel about this? What did he say?"

"I tried many times to get him to agree to make this statue. But he always refused. We were both so stubborn. . . ."

"Well, he must have had certain reasons for not wanting to do it," Sister Dufès continued.

Catherine replied, "It was frustrating for me. I knew our Lady wanted this statue but as long as Father Aladel refused, there was nothing I could do."

"You said there were two things our Lady wanted," said Sister Dufès. "What was the other thing?"

Catherine replied, "Our Lady wanted our chapel on Rue du Bac to be open to everyone. She wants it to be a place of pilgrimage. During the vision, she pointed to the altar and said, 'Come to the foot of *this* altar. There, graces will be poured out on everyone who asks for them with confidence and fervor.'"

Sister Dufès inwardly groaned. *It will be impossible to convince the superiors about this!* she thought. But she said to Catherine, "We'll have to see about that. Only the superiors can do anything about that request."

When Catherine left Sister Dufès was astounded at all she had heard. Sometimes she had looked down on Catherine, taking her for granted. Catherine always did all the hard, heavy work. She didn't claim any special privileges for herself. *All this time, we've been living with such a holy, humble person!* Sister Dufès marveled. *But what am I to do now? How will the superiors react when they hear these requests?* She sat in her chair and thought about it for a long time.

20

THE FINAL ROAD

Sister Dufès lost no time. First, she wrote to Sister Grand (pronounced *ghran*), who had worked with Father Aladel. She might know something about the idea of a statue of Mary holding the globe. A few weeks later, she got a letter back. Sister Grand confirmed it. She had found some notes in Father Aladel's papers about this statue.

In June Sister Dufès went to Rue du Bac with Catherine. Catherine pointed out the exact place where the Blessed Virgin had appeared. Sister Dufès was overjoyed to know more about it.

She wrote to the superiors for permission to have a statue made with Mary holding the globe, so that it could be put in the chapel. But her request was denied. There was already a statue of Mary in the chapel, and they didn't want to have two different representations of Mary in the same place. Also, on the miraculous medal,

Mary is shown holding her hands out. The superiors thought it would be confusing to show her holding the globe.

But Sister Dufès went ahead and had a statue made the way Catherine had described it. She put it in her own office. Catherine was disappointed. Not only would the statue not be put in chapel, but it didn't look anything like the way Mary had appeared! She was also disappointed that the superiors did not want to open the chapel at Rue du Bac to the public. But she resigned herself to it and was consoled to think that she had done what she could.

Catherine was finding it more difficult to get around. She had bad pains in her legs and suffered other health problems. In September 1876, she had to stay in bed and rest for a long time. Her body was growing weaker, but her spirit was as strong as ever.

By October she had gotten better and when she was able, she did whatever work she could. She started to train other sisters to do the things she had done for so long. Catherine seemed to know that her time on earth was drawing to a close. On December 8, the feast of the Immaculate Conception, Catherine went to Rue du Bac. Once again she went to the chapel and relived in her mind the beautiful visions she had seen of Mary.

When it was time to go home, Catherine slipped while she was getting into the carriage. She fell and dislocated her wrist. But she made no fuss about it. She never wanted to draw attention to herself. By this time, Catherine had started telling people that her time on earth was short. "This is the last time I'll celebrate this feast on earth," she said to one of the sisters.

"Don't say things like that!" the other one told her.

"But it is true," Catherine replied. "Soon I will be going to see our Lord and his Blessed Mother."

After that, Catherine's health declined even more. She had to stay in bed most of the time. Christmas came and went. By now Catherine was finding it hard to eat. She took less and less food.

The sisters sensed her time was near. Sister Cosnard (pronounced *KOO-nar*), the sister in charge of teaching the postulants about religious life, came to visit her. Catherine told her, "Tell them to pray well! May the good God inspire our superiors to honor Mary. She is the treasure of our community. Tell everyone to pray the Rosary."

It was December 31, 1876. Catherine was slipping fast. Sister Dufès asked her, "Are you afraid to die?"

Catherine looked at her with some surprise. She said simply, "Why would I be afraid to go and meet our Lord, his Mother, and Saint Vincent?"

The priest brought Holy Communion to Catherine and she received the last sacraments. Catherine was alert. Right to the end, she was always doing things for others. She was preparing small packets of miraculous medals to give to the sisters, as she often liked to do, when suddenly she lost consciousness. The medals fell all over her bed and clattered to the floor. The sisters around her began to pray the prayers for the dying. Catherine rallied again and woke up. But like a candle slowly being consumed, her life was drawing to its close. Slowly and quietly, Catherine slipped away. At seven o'clock in the evening on December 31, Catherine's eyes closed for the last time on earth.

Later that evening, Sister Dufès gathered the community together for a special meeting. "Sisters," she began, "I have something important to tell you. Now that Sister Catherine is gone from us, I can reveal her secret. She is the sister who saw our Lady reveal the miraculous medal!"

Many of the sisters were very surprised. They had never suspected that Catherine was the one. "She was always so humble and hidden!" one of them said.

"Imagine that our Lady came to her!" exclaimed another.

Another sister replied, "Yes, but that is precisely why our Lady came to Sister Catherine. No one was more humble than she."

After that, word spread quickly that Catherine had been the visionary. Large crowds came to her funeral, hoping to see the body of the sister who had seen our Lady.

Only after her death did Catherine's last wishes came true. Eventually a statue of our Lady holding the globe was put in the chapel at Rue du Bac. And the chapel itself was opened to the public. It became a place of pilgrimage. Even today people visit there from all over the world.

Word spread about Catherine's holiness. She wasn't holy just because she saw our Lady. Catherine was holy because of her great love for God and for her neighbors. She spent her life in selfless service of the poor. She lived the words of Saint Vincent, "We can never be happier than when we live and die in the service of the poor."

On July 27, 1947, Pope Pius XII canonized Saint Catherine Labouré. Her feast day is November 28.

Prayer

Saint Catherine, all your life you worked hard. You tried to serve God and love others in simplicity. Even when the Blessed Mother appeared to you and gave you a special mission, you were so humble that many people never guessed what you had experienced. Your special love for the poor moved you to reach out to them, so that they would know how much God loves them. Pray for me that I will have a truly humble heart, grateful for all that God has given me. May I, too, serve God with courage, even when it seems that no one notices.

Mary, our Lady of the Miraculous Medal, you asked Saint Catherine to encourage people to trust in your prayers and help. Pray for me and for all those whom I love. Keep us close to Jesus. O Mary, conceived without sin, pray for us who have recourse to you. Amen.

GLOSSARY

1. **Canonization**—the ceremony in which the pope officially declares that someone is a saint in heaven. To canonize someone is to recognize that he or she has lived a life of heroic virtue, is worthy of imitation, and can intercede for others. Like beatification, which it follows, canonization requires a miracle resulting from the holy person's prayers to God.

2. **Ciborium**—a covered container, usually lined with gold, which contains the consecrated Hosts. It is used for distribution of Holy Communion and afterward is returned to the tabernacle.

3. **Commune**—the name of the temporary government of Paris from March to May 1871. After France lost the Franco-Prussian war, an uprising of workers in Paris resulted in the establishment of the Commune.

4. **Community, religious**—a group of men (priests and brothers) or women (sisters) who are consecrated to God. Each re-

ligious community has its own mission or special work and its own way of praying and living together as a community. Religious priests, brothers, and sisters usually take vows of poverty, chastity, and obedience. Each religious community follows a common rule of life.

5. **Franc**—the type of money used in France until 2002.

6. **Grace**—the gift of God's life within the human soul. Sanctifying grace is the lasting presence of God in us that makes us holy, more like him. We receive sanctifying grace at Baptism. Actual grace is the assistance God offers us during our life to help us to perform good actions. Mary obtains graces from God for us when we ask her to pray for us.

7. **Habit, religious**—a uniform worn by religious sisters, brothers, and priests to identify them as a member of a particular religious institute. A religious habit is a sign of dedication to God and to the Church.

8. **Hospice**—a place where people who are elderly and ill can receive the care that they need.

9. **Last Sacraments**—the sacraments of Reconciliation, Holy Eucharist, and the Anointing of the Sick when they are given to those who are dying. Each of these sacraments gives the sick person the grace needed to prepare well for death and for passage into eternity.

10. **Motherhouse**—the main house of a religious community. A motherhouse is usually located where the community was founded. Often the superior lives in the motherhouse.

11. **Novice**—a person who is in one of the beginning stages of religious life. This stage of prayer and study is a time in which the novice learns more about the religious community and about life as a religious sister, brother, or priest.

12. **Pilgrimage**—a journey to a holy place to venerate a saint or to obtain some spiritual favor. A person making a pilgrimage is called a pilgrim.

13. **Postulant**—a person who has just entered a religious community and is in the beginning stage of religious life. This stage of prayer and study is called postulancy.

14. **Relics**—a saint's body (or part of it), something closely connected to the saint, or something that touched the body of the saint. They are placed in shrines and in containers called reliquaries.

15. **Religious life**—a state of life in which men and women are consecrated to God and try to follow Jesus. Religious men and women make vows, live together, and follow a rule in the spirit of their congregation's founder.

16. **Spiritual director**—a person who gives guidance in the spiritual life and how to grow closer to God.

17. **Superior, religious**—the person who has authority in a religious community. The superior's authority is described in the rules of the religious community and in the laws of the Church.

18. **Vincentians**—a community of priests and brothers, officially the Congregation of the Mission. The Vincentians were founded by Saint Vincent de Paul to evangelize through preaching, religious instruction, and formation.

19. **Vocation**—the call of God for a person to become holy through a certain way of life. One can be called to marriage, single life, the ordained life of a priest or deacon, or the religious life. Everyone is called to holiness.

20. **Vow**—an important promise freely made to God. Members of religious communities take three vows: poverty, chastity, and obedience. Members of the Daughters of Charity take a fourth vow to serve persons who are poor, sick, and in need.

Who are the Daughters of St. Paul?

We are Catholic sisters. Our mission is to be like Saint Paul and tell everyone about Jesus! There are so many ways for people to communicate with each other. We want to use all of them so everyone will know how much God loves them. We do this by printing books (you're holding one!), making radio shows, singing, helping people at our bookstores, using the Internet, and in many other ways.

Visit our website at www.pauline.org

BOOKS & MEDIA

The Daughters of St. Paul operate book and media centers at the following addresses. Visit, call or write the one nearest you today, or find us on the World Wide Web, www.pauline.org.

CALIFORNIA
3908 Sepulveda Blvd, Culver City, CA 90230   310-397-8676
935 Brewster Ave., Redwood City, CA 94063   650-369-4230
5945 Balboa Avenue, San Diego, CA 92111   858-565-9181

FLORIDA
145 S.W. 107th Avenue, Miami, FL 33174   305-559-6715

HAWAII
1143 Bishop Street, Honolulu, HI 96813   808-521-2731
Neighbor Islands call: 866-521-2731

ILLINOIS
172 North Michigan Avenue, Chicago, IL 60601   312-346-4228

LOUISIANA
4403 Veterans Memorial Blvd, Metairie, LA 70006   504-887-7631

MASSACHUSETTS
885 Providence Hwy, Dedham, MA 02026   781-326-5385

MISSOURI
9804 Watson Road, St. Louis, MO 63126   314-965-3512

NEW YORK
64 West 38th Street, New York, NY 10018   212-754-1110

PENNSYLVANIA
Philadelphia—relocating   215-676-9494

SOUTH CAROLINA
243 King Street, Charleston, SC 29401   843-577-0175

VIRGINIA
1025 King Street, Alexandria, VA 22314   703-549-3806

CANADA
3022 Dufferin Street, Toronto, ON M6B 3T5   416-781-9131